Sexual Pleasure in Intercourse

Hari Datt Sharma

V&S PUBLISHERS

Published by:

V&S PUBLISHERS

F-2/16, Ansari Road, Daryaganj, New Delhi-110002
☎ 011-23240026, 011-23240027 • *Fax* 011-23240028
Email info@vspublishers.com • *Website* www.vspublishers.com

Regional Office Hyderabad
5-1-707/1, Brij Bhawan (Beside Central Bank of India Lane)
Bank Street, Koti, Hyderabad - 500 095
☎ 040-24737290
E-mail vspublishershyd@gmail.com

Branch Office Mumbai
Jaywant Industrial Estate, 2nd Floor–222, Tardeo Road
Opposite Sobo Central Mall, Mumbai – 400 034
☎ 022-23510736
E-mail: vspublishersmum@gmail.com

Follow us on: 🇹 🇫 🇮🇳

All books available at **www.vspublishers.com**

Contents

Preface

The fact that sex is of fundamental importance, can hardly be overemphasised. Sex is the very foundation of existence. Yet pleasure is the basic necessity needs our attention.

The basic sex drive is a universal experience, but what turns people on, differs from culture to culture. Sex still makes some people feel uncomfortable and embarrassed partly because it has been associated for so long with unacceptable and dirty feelings. Sniggering is sometimes a way of covering up these feelings. Embarrassment also comes from the secrecy surrounding the sexual act. Secrets mean you have done something wrong. In societies where sex has been open and free from ideas of guilt; it is accepted much more easily as being normal and natural.

A person may be a millionaire, a world leader, an athlete, a wrestler or a distinguished scientist—but still feels inadequate doing a simple act of sex that is common for animals and birds. It is because animals and birds never think about it. They just respond to changing levels of sex hormones which stimulate or curb their reproductive urge. But in the case of men and women, instincts have been crippled by anxiety resulting from negative preconditioning normally based on expectations of family and norms of the society.

The logic of the various religious leaders is that because sex is necessary to keep the human race going, therefore the sole purpose of sex is reproduction. But it is not accepted by all. You might as well say that since food is necessary to keep the body going, the sole purpose of eating is to stay alive, which won't convince anyone who enjoys rich foods.

If the only purpose of sex were reproduction, nature would have arranged for human females to come on heat only once a year which is sufficient to reproduce the species. While a great deal of sexual activities directly or indirectly relate to reproduction, but having children is not the only purpose of sexual activities. Sex provides release from tension. Sex is stimulating. Any satisfactory sexual experience heightens perception, alleviates boredom and awakens new interests.

Sex offers companionship and intimacy as most of us are afraid of loneliness. Sex can also be used as a weapon. Desired behaviour can be coerced by withholding sex as a punishment or offering it as a reward. Sex is also a form of recreation, available to all classes and conditions of people throughout the world. Pornography, blue movies and dirty jokes are significant form of entertainment. Sex can also be used as an inducement to buy or sell. With such a powerful medium at our disposal, we surely owe it to ourselves to know as much about it as possible.

How you enjoy sex is also a matter of personal preference and is no one else's business. Just as no two people have exactly the same taste in food or clothes, so no two people like exactly the same thing in bed. Perversion is the name we give to other people's variations; to our own we call preference.

For good sex, we need a relaxed and comfortable setting, plenty of good feelings, self-esteem, placing a higher value on own worth. It is a quality which is particularly likely to develop with age and is absolutely necessary for good sexual relationship. But with an increase in number of sexually transmitted diseases, it is necessary for the readers to differentiate between the rights and the wrongs.

Gone are the days when men had to put up with log-like stiff partners. It is now accepted that educated girls have sexual appetites every bit as large as those of men, and have every right to have them satisfied. So, it is not surprising that men feel the pressure on them to perform.

I am sure this book will entirely change your attitude towards sex, and will prove to be an informative, educative and enjoyable reading material for you.

Hari Datt Sharma

Male Sex Organs

Research findings show that some men suffer from an emotional concern that they possess a penis that is abnormally small, a concern based in part on the individual's visual perceptive when looking downwards a flaccid penis, a viewpoint that distorts the true size. The complex may also be supported by the emphasis in literature and other art forms as well as folklore and pornographic material on male genitals that are unusually large.

Myths about the Size of the Penis

Penises vary greatly in shape and it is a myth that a bigger penis is necessarily better. One of the cherished illusions men have about their sexual performance is that the bigger their penis, the better they will satisfy their partner. It is an illusion nourished by pulp fictions and girlie magazines.

The kind of men they read about in novels and stories have penis as hard as iron and as long as a barber's pole, always ready for action. As soon as the penis loses an erection, there is another one raring to go. In these stories, rarely do people come across floppy or remarkably small penises, the kind that droop a little and need coaxing to come into action. Stories of sex with animals by women also confirm their belief in this myth.

The Reality about the Size of the Penis

Despite all the fears and boasts, penis size does not vary markedly from one person to another. There are some large penises around, just as there are some men whose erection can last a long time and return after a short time. But there is far less difference than is generally supposed.

Circumcision

It is a minor operation to remove the foreskin from the man's or boy's penis. This is done for religious reason among Muslim community or sometimes for medical reasons.

Does it make one a better lover if one has been circumcised?

People often think that men who have been circumcised cannot control ejaculation.

Another view is that a circumcised person can continue for longer duration of sexual act than a non-circumcised person. But both these views are myths. During erection, the foreskin usually draws back from the sensitive glans (the head of the penis). So at this stage it is hard to tell if someone has been circumcised.

Being circumcised or not, it makes no difference to the sexual enjoyment.

Small Penis Complex

Sex researchers have found that penises vary in length between 5 to 10 cm when limp, but when they are erect they all average at about 15 cm. Those, that are smaller when relaxed, increase in size more than larger ones. In other words with erection, the difference tends to level out. One erect penis is much the same size as every one else's.

.The Size of the Penis Makes no Difference to Sexual Enjoyment

Forget everything you have been told about penis size. Even if it is undersized, even then it can satisfy the woman better than a big penis. Some men are so obsessed with the idea "bigger is better" that they do not feel adequate even though they are normal. It is now firmly established beyond doubt that penis size makes no difference to women's sexual enjoyment.

Chromosomal Anomalies

About one male in a thousand has a penis which is unusually small due to a chromosomal anomality. It may have XX rather than XY chromosome sets. In medical language it is known as **Klinefelter's Syndrome**. The extra chromosome means that such individual usually develops feminine breasts and has a low sperm count. They also tend to be obese and display a low level of sexual interest.

There is no relation between **penis size** and **body size**. However there are slight racial differences. Orientals on average have smaller penises than Caucasians. Negroes have larger penises.

However plastic surgeons who perform penis enlargement, report a flourishing business. The results report extension of about one to two inches. It entails releasing the penile shaft from the ligaments and drawing a flap of skin from the pubic area to cover the added length. But it is not worth the time, trouble, money and pain suffered in this connection.

Quacks often Dupe the People

As most people worry about the size of their penis, so charlatans exploit this situation very well to their own advantage. They easily and gladly separate fools from their money for medically approved apparatus or techniques that promise to enlarge penis. Indian quacks prescribe strange types of medicines like massage of the penis with the special oil prepared from a type of lizard *(Sandey-Ka-Tel)*. It is just to befool the people. It does more harm than good.

All the techniques and apparatuses prove ineffective and at worst they can be harmful. Some vacuum like devices can rupture blood vessels in the penis. Sex findings indicate that no pill, potion, exercise, masturbatory technique or external device can affect penis size.

My advice is—Don't worry, feel happy. Your penis is quite normal. When any man who feels anxiety about his penis and reluctantly or hesitantly engages himself in sexual play, the result is the lack of satisfaction.

In evaluating himself, a man must take into consideration his genital inheritance and what physical characteristics his parents and grand-parents handed down to him.

Anatomy of Male Sex Organ

The sex apparatus in a man is only an exterior limb. It is more visible than woman's. The penis is generally less cloaked in mystery. This can be both an advantage as

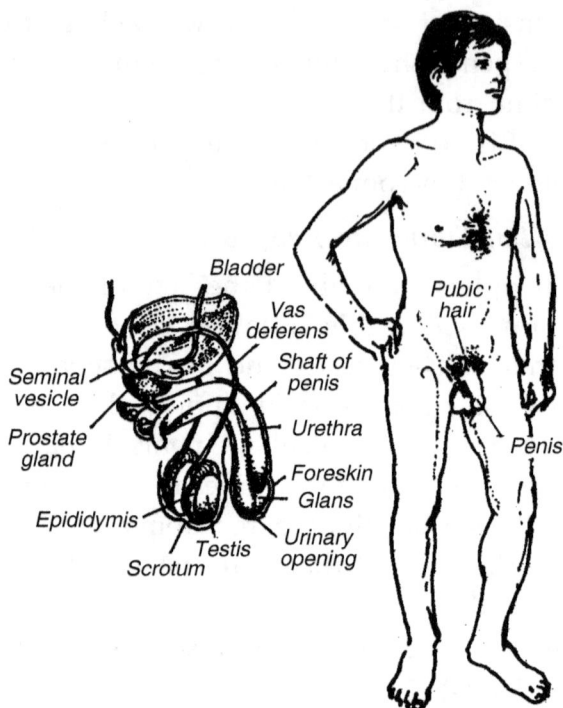

Male reproductive system

well as disadvantage. Penises have an annoying habit of becoming erect at the wrong time and refusing to do so at the right time. They also cause a great deal of anxiety to their owners because of their shape or size.

The biological sexual function of the penis is to penetrate the female vagina and deposit sperm. It is also the urinary outlet. Generally it remains flacid but in response to erotic stimuli it becomes erect and engorged with blood. Erection increases its length and girth. The erection and softening of a penis are fascinating to watch. Both can be brought on by various physical and mental stimuli, but neither is routinely under voluntary control.

Normally it hangs limply downward, but in its erect state it points horizontally outward or slightly upwards at an angle. A penis has no muscles along its length, nor any bone, just a ring of muscles around the base which tightens during sexual excitement and helps to keep it erect.

The Penis

The penis is made up of a long shaft and sensitive tip which is called **glans**. The glans has an opening in it. This is the opening of the **urethra**, a narrow tube which performs the dual function of carrying urine from the bladder and semen from the **vas deferens**—the tube which leads from the **testes**. But it never performs both the functions at the same time. During erection, a small muscle closes off the entrance to the bladder so that no urine can be passed. So it is not possible to pass urine and ejaculate at the same time.

The shaft is covered with loose, wrinkly darkish skin which extends over tip to form the foreskin. The head is studded with a mass of nerve ending which make it the most sensitive part of the penis. The whole of the rim or ridge where the head joins the shaft is capable of providing some very pleasant sensations.

On the underside of the shaft is an exquisitely sensitive area the **ferrum**, which looks like a tightly stretched bowstring. Even the lightest touch applied to this part of the penis is enough to produce an erection.

Scrotum and Testes

The loose pouch of wrinkled skin which hangs down behind the penis and which contains the testes is called the Scrotal sack or Scrotum. It has slightly coarse, slightly hairy skin.

The testes produce sperms and testosterone, the hormone responsible for the sex drive. The testes can only produce sperms at a temperature of 35⁰C, which is 2⁰C cooler than the temperature inside our body. Each testis contains about 100 m long tiny coiled tube. Sperms are made inside these tubes from puberty until well into old age. When a man ejaculates, replacement sperms are made in these testes. These tubes also transport sperm-laden semen to vas deferens, which are muscular tubes. They are about 40 cm long. When a man ejaculates, sperms are squeezed through these tubes and out of the penis.

About a teaspoonful of semen that comes out, carries almost 400 million sperms. Nature makes sure that atleast one sperm reaches the egg.

Myths about the Testicles

Many men assume that the size of testicles influences sexual power and performance. Normal testicles do not depend upon size or shape. Most men have two testicles but some men have one non-descended testicle and they are able to function perfectly well. Sex drive is mainly influenced by thought patterns and not by the anatomical shape of any organ. Both testicles are never the same. Mostly one hangs lower than the other.

Being Normal

Most people have doubts about themselves in one way or another. If you think you are not normal, your body will not function normally. In 99% of cases, when people believe that something is wrong with them, it is a fact that their problem is psychological rather than physical. In sexual matters we seem to be obsessed with being normal.

A person may be a rich man or may be a distin-guished leader—but still feel inadequate in a simple act of sex that is common for animals and birds. This difference is due to negative preconditioning, concerning our normally based expectations of family and society.

Other Factors

80% of men have erection problems periodically. It is normal.

20% of men are bothered about premature ejaculation, due to lack of control.

10% of men have difficulty reaching orgasm and ejaculating semen.

If a man is able to satisfy the woman of his choice in any way that they mutually decide, he can consider himself normal.

❑❑

Semen is the Seed of the Man

Earth is the essence of the elements,
Water is the essence of the earth,
Plants are the essence of the water,
Flowers are the essence of plants,
Fruits are the essence of flowers,
Man is the essence of the fruits,
Semen is the seed of the man.

(From *Udgith* in the Chandogya Upanishad)

Semen

Semen is a milky, sticky liquid. It is made of **Seminal Fluid,** released from the **Prostate Gland,** and **Seminal Vesicles.** It contains millions of sperms. About a teaspoonful of semen contains about 400 million sperms. As semen contains sperms, so, a woman can get pregnant if she has unprotected sexual intercourse with a man. During puberty some boys wake up at night to find semen coming out of their penis. Or boys wake up in the morning and find semen on their pyjamas or sheets. This means that they have had a *nocturnal emission* (wet dream).

Semen Myths

Throughout the world many fictitious beliefs and superstitions are prevailing concerning semen. Hindu religious leaders preach that the semen is the basis of health, strength and life, therefore, semen should be preserved and conserved through abstinence. Masturbation and nocturnal emissions are very harmful hence these should be avoided. That is why *Brahamcharya* has found a prominent place in the Hindu religious thinking.

Hindu belief is based on this conception that after eating 32 kg of food 800 gm blood is formed and out of that blood only 20 gm semen is formed. That means, if you have wasted 20 gm semen through masturbation or nocturnal emission, you have wasted the benefits of 32 kg food.

Early Chinese also held that ejaculation diminished the male element and therefore reduced the man's strength and may even shorten his life. Therefore various methods were used to retain as much semen as possible even during intercourse.

In early Tantric and Taoist Treatises the use of various techniques are suggested to regulate and control the emission of semen, so that it may ascend and nourish the brain. For this purpose a number of breath and thought control methods are suggested.

Such religious thinking helps the quacks to dupe the people of their hard earned money.

Role of the Scrotum and Testes in Producing Semen

The scrotum is a loose pouch of wrinkled darkish skin in which two testes of oval bodies are enclosed. The left testicle is slightly lower of the two and the whole structure is asymmetrical. In normal proportion the centre of the scrotum should reach lower down than the tip of the slack penis. There is no fatty layer. There are involuntary muscular tissues under the skin which contract in response to various stimuli. For instance, if they get too hot, the scrotum drops slightly so that the testes can cool down.

The scrotum is divided by a partition, in which the muscles are joined together and each division contains one testicle and one epididymis. Epididymis are two thin coiled tubules, which store the sperms that have been made in the testes. Sperms are formed in the testicles.

The mature testicle is 4 to 4½ cm long; at the utmost it does not exceed 5 cm. It is 2 to 3 cm broad and weighs between 15 to 26 gm.

The testicles are the parts of male reproductive system. The testicle on the left side is larger than the one on the right side. The two male testes hang down behind the penis. The nerves and blood-vessels enter the organs from behind. Besides this each testicle is joined and clasped from the back by the epididymis—an oval pad cushion. The head of the epididymis is fastened to the upper pole or extremity of the testicle and the two structures are closely interconnected.

The testicles are divided internally by a regular pattern of partitions into paramidical cups or cells. In each of these is a cluster of very minute curved and intertwined tubules, in which the spermatozoa, or sperm cells are formed. The testes produce the male sex hormone, *testosterone* which causes the changes in the body during puberty.

Hanging Scrotum

The reason why scrotum hang outside the body is that sperms are best produced at one or two degrees lower than the normal body temperature. The testes can only produce sperm at a temperature of 35 C, which is 2 degrees cooler than the temperature inside the body. If it is cooler outside, the skin of the scrotum shrinks, drawing the testes up towards the body for warmth. If they get too hot, the scrotum drops slightly so that the testes can cool down.

Sperm Cells

The production of sperm cells goes on in man from puberty to advanced old age at the rate of 500 million a day during peak production. The cells are termed seminal cells. A sperm looks a bit like a tadpole with a head, neck and a tail. The head transmits the qualities of genus and individual. The neck acts as oar to sweep the sperm forwards. These sperms come into motion when they are blended with a liquid secretion of the vesicles and prostate gland but in the testicles they remain motionless.

Only 200 to 300 million sperms are ejaculated at any one time. In fact, up to 100 million sperms can mature in just 24 hours.

Sperms Reach their Destination

Apart from the independent motion of the individual sperm cells, they are also driven forward and onward in the testicles by the accumulation of secretion, and gradual muscular apparatus of these ducts. They cover the last stage through the urethra with lightning speed and impetus in the ejaculation. If a man is having unprotected sexual intercourse with a woman and his penis is inside her vagina when he ejaculates, the sperm can swim through the woman's cervix into her uterus and travel up her fallopian tubes. If a single sperm meets a mature ovum here and joins with it, conception takes place.

Out of 200 to 500 million sperms that enter the vagina at the time of coitus only one is fortunate enough to enter the ovum. Others are expelled out by the vaginal secretions, which are too acidic to suit them as a medium. But the slight acidity of the vaginal secretions, at certain period of the cycle, and the distinctly alkaline spermatic fluid of uterine and tubular secretions, on the other hand, are very congenial to the sperms.

A man produces as much sperms as are needed. If he is not ejaculating due to masturbation or sexual intercourse, the production of the sperms slows down.

Function of the Prostate Gland

The prostate gland is a part of reproductive system. It surrounds the male urethra and is about the size of a golf ball.

During the spasmodic contractions or convulsion at the moment of sexual intercourse, this powerful muscular apparatus is able to squeeze and force the secretions it contains into the urethra. The ducts in which these secretions are formed are about thirty in number, and open-close together at the same place, in the urethral wall where the two seminal ducts also join the urethra.

The specific secretion of the prostate gland forms a milky-white, thin alkaline fluid containing sperms. These prostatic secretions are forced into the Urethra together with the sperm secretions from the testicles. Prostate secretion forms a large proportion of the ejaculate or discharge. Their alkalinity preserves the sperms and stimulates their mobility.

The length of the spermatic cord is about 45 cm. This length makes it a much more effective suction pump for the testicular products. This length also makes it able to contain a large amount of such secretions, so that throughout it may serve as a **reservoir**, as well as a conduit or duct. In the reservoir there are compartments in which the seminal fluid from the epididymis collects. Main storage of the semen takes place in the reservoir. When these are overfull the vesicles act as safety valves and extra containers.

The vesicular product is a tough, yellowish and sticky substance which gets mixed up in the seminal fluid.

Ejaculation

When the accumulated tension as a result of brimming seminal fluid in the reservoir and vesicles—has passed a certain limit, the involuntary muscles of these organs contract automatically in strong spasms. Then drive their fluid contents in tiny columns of spray against the anterior urethral wall. At the same time the prostatic muscles contract, and project the special secretions of the prostate gland into the urethra. It is a reflex action produced during copulation or masturbation and the sensation associated with it is also called **orgasm**.

Urethral Crest

It is not possible for the seminal fluid to flow away inwards in the direction of the bladder. And simultaneously it becomes impossible for the urine to pass with and get mixed into the semen, so long as the penis is in erection. The urethral crest makes it impossible to pass water or urine.

Penis after Ejaculation

After ejaculation, blood flows from the spongy tissue of the penis at a faster rate than fresh arterial blood flown in until the penis is flaccid again. Further stimulation persists and causes a renewal of the process once again.

Empty Reservoir and Vesicles

It is difficult to tell whether reservoirs and vesicles become entirely empty after ejaculation. But we find that it is possible to repeat coitus almost at once, so, we can assume that only a partial emptying of these organs takes place.

It is also true that complete or partial discharge is a matter of individual's particular way of thinking. That is why one man can only have coitus once on each occasion, and another several times in rapid succession.

But only a thin fluid is finally discharged which contains mostly prostatic secretion but no sperms or at most very few. For example, animals like cattle, sheeps and stallions etc. have reservoirs like man and so they perform coitus very quickly. However dogs and cats have no reservoirs and they are compelled to depend on vas deferens for their supply in coitus and hence take comparatively longer time.

Emmission of Sperms

In one ejaculation between 5 and 10 ml of semen is discharged containing about 60 million spermatozoa. When emission occurs in rapid succession, both quantity and quality diminish.

Longevity of Sperms

Once sperms have become fully developed at the man's reproductive organs, their life-span depends on where they happen to be. Mature sperms can be stored in the seminal vesicles for several weeks before they are reabsorbed as waste by the body. The ideal condition for the survival of sperm is a moist, warm, alkaline environment—such as found within the uterus. Here after intercourse, sperms can live for up to three days. Before ejaculation sperm's longevity can be measured in weeks and months.

Length of the Tube that Produces Sperms

Each testis contains about 100 metre of thread-like tubes in which sperms are made and transported to vas deferens.

Sperm Duct

Vas deferens is one of the two muscular tubes that join the testes to the ejaculatory duct via prostate gland. It carries spermatozoa to the urethra on ejaculation aided by contraction of its muscular wall.

Odour in the Semen

The prostate fluid which gets mixed in the semen cuases odour. This odour does not come from testicular secretion.

Composition of Man's Semen

The average one teaspoonful of semen contains, along with protein in the sperm, the sugar fructose, ascorbic acid, small amount of zinc and traces of cholesterol. It has calorific value of a raw carrot.

Swallowing Semen

Swallowing semen is absolutely harmless and might even have some nutritional value. But due to childhood taboos, many people are afraid of their natural secretion.

□□

Female Sex Organs

Uterus

Uterus is a part of the female reproductive system. It is also called womb. It is a hollow muscular organ with thick walls located in the pelvic region of the female, the structure in which a fertilized ovum is nurtured into a viable individual. In a non-pregnant woman the uterus is a small pear shaped organ about 7 cm in length which protrudes at the cervical end into the vault of the vagina. Two fallopian tubes, or oviducts are attached to the uterus at both sides less than 2.5 cm from the top or fundus. The portion below the level of the tubes is the body of the uterus. All girls are born with a uterus.

Each month as part of the menstrual cycle, the lining of the uterus thickens in case an ovum is fertilized by a sperm. If the ovum is not fertilized, the thickened endometrium breaks down and pass out of the girl's or woman's vagina as her menstrual period. When the oavum is fertilized and the woman is pregnant, the uterus contains the unborn baby. It has to stretch a lot to make room for the baby to grow. By the time the baby is ready to be born, the uterus may be more than 50 cm long from top to bottom. During labour, muscles in the uterus tighten and relax in order to pull the cervix open so that the baby can pass out of the uterus. After the baby is born, the uterus starts to return to its normal size.

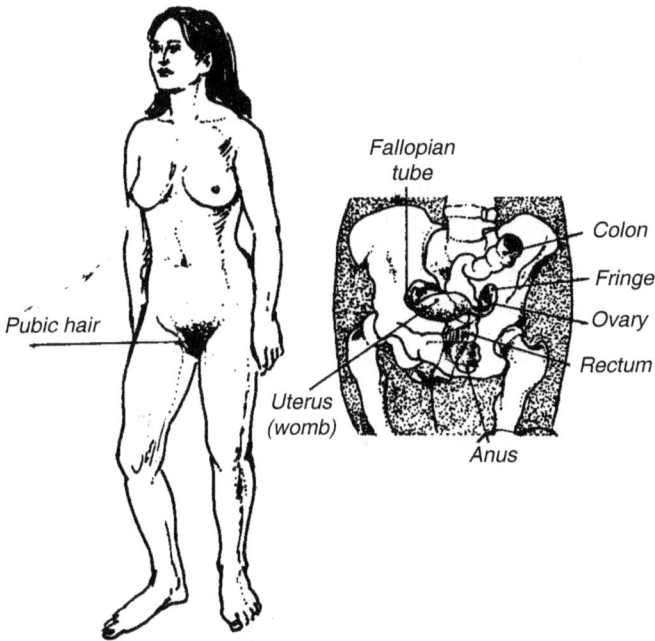

Female reproductive system

Vagina

Vagina is also a part of the female reproductive system. The vagina is a muscular tube inside a woman's body which connects her uterus to the outside of her body. It is about 10 cm long. The walls of the vagina are made up of soft folds of skin. The vagina is located anatomically between the bladder and the rectum and is supported by ligaments and muscles of the pelvic floor. Its walls are formed by an internal mucous membrane lining and a muscular coat, with an erectile tissue between them.

The main functions of the vagina are to provide passageway for spermatozoa from the penis to reach uterus. It is also an outlet for the menstrual flow from the uterus, and a birth canal for the foetus. The vaginal lining responds to stimulation by the female sex hormones

Oestrogen and **Progesterone**. This lining is continuous with uterus but it is not smooth surface. It is marked with furrows and ridges. These are called columns of vagina. The inside of the vagina can be dry or wet.

The empty vagina in a state of sexual response has an average length of 8 to 10 cm. At the time of coitus, penetration does not take place upto the root. This only occurs in certain special positions.

Vulva

Vulva is the name given to a woman's outer sex organ. After puberty it will have pubic hair growing there. The labia majora, the labia minora, the clitoris, the vestibules or opening of the vagina are the parts of the vulva.

Clitoris

It is the most sensitive part of the female genitals. The clitoris is where the inner labia meets at the front of the vulva. Only the tip of the clitoris is visible, and is covered by a hood or fold of skin.

The clitoris is full of nerve endings and when it is stimulated it becomes stiff like an erect penis and pokes out of its hood. Stimulating the clitoris helps many women to have an orgasm. The clitoris is, in fact, the **power house** of a woman's sexual feelings. It does not play any part in reproduction except to make sex play more pleasurable.

Like the penis, it has a suspensory ligament and two small muscles, which during sexual arousal are engorged by blood and become fuller and firmer. When this happens, the hood pulls back and exposes the delicate tip. But at the peak of excitement it shrinks back into its hood again. The clitoris may be stimulated directly by stroking the shaft slowly and gently to begin with and then faster and with a firm touch as excitement mounts.

During intercourse the pressure of the man's pubic bone against the clitoris may be sufficient stimulation for some women. For others the tugging action of the penis on the whole vulval area does the trick. But a large number of women need direct and continuous stimulation of the clitoris by hand at the time of penetration in order to reach orgasm. Typically, women like clitoral stimulation to be part of a total involvement and not to be seen like an obligation. It should be slow and soft at first, gradually building more pressure and speed. A technique frequently preferred is that stimulation should start with whole hand massage and then use only one or two fingers.

Labia

The word labia means lips. There are two types of labia— the outer labia and the inner labia.

The Outer Labia—These are also called labia majora. They are two pieces of thick skin that surround the vaginal orifice. These are shaped like a pair of lips and they consist of longitudinal folds of tissue that extend downwards and backwards from the mons pubis, enclosing the labia minora, the vagina, the urethra and the clitoris. The labia majora becomes wider and engorged with blood during sexual excitement. Pubic hair grows over the outer labia of the girls who have reached puberty. The outer labia are generally closed so that they can protect the more delicate parts underneath them such as the Vagina and the Clitoris.

The Inner Labia—The inner labia are also called labia minora. These are thinner than the outer labia and they can be seen when the outer labia are parted. They are sensitive to touch. As in the case of the labia majora, they also swell during sexual excitements. They come together in the prepuce of the clitoris at the upper end and in the hymen at the lower end.

Pubic Hair

Hair growth in the pubic region is one of the first signs of puberty. On the onset of puberty a patch of hair appears just above the genitals in a male and a female. The hair may vary in density, size and colour from person to person. This is considered to be a secondary sex characteristic. Even the sight of pubic hair is exciting to most men and some women.

Hymen

It is a very thin layer or membrane of skin which covers part of the vaginal opening. Every girl's hymen is different. Some women have hymens which look complete but which contain enough tiny holes to let menstrual blood flow through, when they have their menstrual period.

This delicate membrane stretches over the entrance of the vagina closing it partially. Many women have large opening in the hymen and some have no hymen at all.

Some religious and cultural groups expect a woman to have a complete hymen when she gets married. This is because one way in which a hymen is broken is through intercourse. If her hymen is broken, she is not considered as virgin. But this conception is not in conformity with fact.

For instance, those girls who ride a horse or a bike or do a lot of sports, gym or dancing, the hymen may get ruptured. By using a tampon in the vagina also hymen can be broken.

During the first act of intercourse, the hymen is normally torn, or atleast perforated, in two places on right and left. This penetration is accompanied by a slight loss of blood. It is almost always painful to a greater or lesser degree. In women over 30 years of age it is hard and tough and offers considerable difficulties in coitus.

Various cultures foster the myth that all first instances of hymenal penetration are painful and show bleeding. To accommodate these expectations, women often feign pain and discomfort and ensure the presence of blood stains. A woman or her mother may see to it that some blood stains are visible.

Perineum

The area between a woman's labia and her anus is called perineum. When a woman has a baby, her perineum has to stretch until it is very thin. It might even tear or have to be cut to let the baby through. However, in the case of a man the region between the anus and scrotum is called Perinial. It is through this area that any treatment or diagnosis of the prostate is carried out.

Cervix

Cervix is the neck of the uterus and a passageway between the uterine cavity and the vagina. In a woman who has never been pregnant, the cervix is almost conical in shape. It protrudes from the uterus into the vault of the vagina. It is closed during pregnancy to contain the foetus but opens during **labour** so that the baby can leave the uterus and be pushed out through the vagina.

Fallopian Tube

There are two fallopian tubes or oviducts. They are muscular tubes, one on each side of the uterus. Every month as part of the menstrual cycle, an ovum is released by one ovary into the fallopian tube nearest to it. If a woman has sexual intercourse with a man around this time, the ovum may be fertilized by a sperm in the fallopian tube. As the ovum moves through the fallopian tube, it is most likely to encounter spermatozoa about halfway along the route to the uterus, the usual site of fertilization. However, any obstruction or lesion in fallopian tubes can be a reason of sterility.

Fimbria

The outer ends of the fallopian tubes are called fimbria. When ovulation takes place and an ovum is released, the fimbria sweep the ovum into the fallopian tube.

Ovary

Ovary is the part of female reproductive system. Women have two ovaries, one on each side of the uterus. They are attached to the uterus by fibres. They are oval in shape and about 4 cm long and 1 cm wide. In girls who have reached puberty, the ovaries take it in turns to release an ovum each month and to produce female sex hormones **Oestrogen** and **Progesterone** which are responsible for some of the changes which take place during the menstrual cycle. During puberty these hormones help reproductive organs grow and develop. The ovaries stop releasing ova after the menopause.

Ovum

The female sex cell or egg cell is called ovum. An ovum is so small that it can't be seen without a microscope. The ovum travels down the fallopian tube and if it meets a man's sperm, it is fertilized and it lodges itself in the woman's uterus and starts to develop into a baby. If it is not fertilized, it passes out of the woman's vagina in her vaginal fluid. Girls are born with 4 lakhs ovas stored in their ovaries. But only about 300 to 500 are released during a woman's fertile years between puberty and the menopause. The remaining disintegrate.

❑❑

Techniques of Sexual Intercourse

Indian love manuals describe a number of techniques for sexual intercourse. The 4th century Hindu classic known as **Kama Sutra** and of 15th century **Ananga Ranga** are full of such descriptions.

Love making does not necessarily begin when the man inserts his penis into the woman's vagina. This action is just one stage.

William Masters and Virginia Johnson of USA, in their book "Human Sexual Response", said that the physiology of man and woman engaged in love making can be divided into four phases—Excitement, Plateau, Orgasm and Resolution.

The Excitement Phase

It begins for the man in the form of penile erection and for the woman with clitoral erection. Nerves in the organs cause valves in the erectile tissue to close, trapping blood, producing swelling, and heightening sensitivity. Both men and women experience an increase in heart beats and breathing rates and an elevation of blood pressure. The nipples of both stand out, swell and become more sensitive.

In women, the labia majora open and spread flat, while the labia minora swell and extend outward. The clitoris steadily increases in length and diameter. She starts to produce more vaginal fluid and her labia begins to feel quite wet and that serves as a lubricant during sexual excitement.

The uterus and cervix pull back away from the vagina, leaving more room for the deposit of semen. The entire length of the vagina expands somewhat, but the inner two-thirds open more to create a channel that is ready to receive the penis. Parts of the female body flush darker in colour especially the labia.

In men, the penis begins to engorge with blood which makes its spongy tissue to expand. It grows longer and thicker and becomes stiff and upright. The nerves in the penis receive further stimulation from the gonads. Another automatic reflex increases the blood flow even more. The spongy mass around the urethra swells and presses against its sheath of skin, stretching the sheath to its maximum. The penis increases in circumference by at least two and a half times. The penis continues to stay just slightly upward until ejaculation is accomplished.

Meanwhile, the testes are pulled in even closer to the body by contraction of the attaching tendons and muscles. The scrotal sack shrinks to maintain this condition for a long period, although the condition may be lost and regained repeatedly without orgasm.

Most penises are equal in action, no matter how large or small they are, the vagina is impartial and recognises few distinctions of the length and breadth of a penis. No man should think himself as sexual superior of his fellowman merely because he is endowed with a greater penis.

The Plateaue Phase

In the plateaue phase, the testes draw still closer to the body as excitement increases and the level of tension develops. There is a specific elevation of both testes towards the perineum. As male sexual tension rises through plateaue phase towards orgasmic phase release, the specific reaction of testicular elevation progresses until the pre-ejaculatory, positioning in tight opposition to the male ejaculation is attained.

The plateau phase is a continuation of the effects of stimulation, with the reaction becoming stronger and more constant. Breathing quickens. The penis increases slightly in diameter near its tip. The opening into the urethra from which the semen will ejaculate becomes more slit like. The tip and the head of the penis change colour to a deeper reddish purple. Finally the erection is intensified to the point of completion, and involuntary nervous tension is so strong that the organ goes into tiny muscular spasms.

The penis provides its own lubrication by releasing small amount of semen containing sperm. Even without physical manipulation the lubricating ejaculate may drip from the penis.

If the penis is in the woman's vagina at this moment, even if neither partner experiences any sensation closer to orgasm, and sperms are deposited—no matter how few—can cause pregnancy.

For females, the inner two-thirds of the vagina balloons, while the outer third narrows to about half its excitement—phase in diameter. This helps the vaginal muscles both to grasp the penis more effectively and to produce a slight vacuum to suction out the seminal fluid.

The vagina, after all, has been fashioned by nature to act as a repository of the stuff for survival of the species. In the plateau phase the vaginal vault resembles a fennel, with the penis inserted in the narrow end and the sperms cradled in the wide end.

The inner lips of the woman's labia minora now become a brighter red, as they become congested with blood. More fluid "sweats" through the vaginal walls for lubrication wetness is felt between the legs. Inside the uterus which had begun to elevate during the excitement phase, now elevates fully; the muscles contract in the abdomen, around the groin, and through the buttock region. Both the pulse and breathing are fast, and a "sex flush" appears on certain parts of the body.

The man too is nearing the end of the plateau phase better described as the pre-ejaculatory phase.

The Orgasm Phase

The peak of sexual excitement is called orgasm. In the orgasm phase, the heart rates elevate to anywhere between 140 to 180 beats per minute while the normal rate is around 70 per minute. The genital muscles of both partners go through a patterned series of contraction. In fact all the muscles of their bodies react much like the genitals by contracting, the buttocks tighten, eyes close, and skin tingles.

The belief that all women have multiple orgasm is a myth. While females are physically capable of multiple orgasm, they are not likely to experience them often and many may not even want them.

Another myth is that if intercourse is right it results in simultaneous orgasm. It is just a happy coincidence and not a result of the right technique. A woman may not climax at all—despite this, many women feel satisfying sexual pleasure from having a man's penis inside them, and from watching how the man gets lost in the orgasmic experience.

An orgasm for a man occurs when the muscles around the urethra go through a number of rapid, involuntary contractions. These contractions begin at the back of the penis and in the genital area and move forward along the line of the urethra. Near the end of the plateau phase, semen that has gathered within the head of the penis is pumped to the top of the urethra to force the semen out through the penile opening.

Ejaculation is accompanied by three or four strong bursts each lasting about eight-tenths seconds, with each burst separated by same amount of time. On the average about three and a half millilitres of semen is ejaculated which is less than one teaspoon. The quantity diminishing with each repeated ejaculation. Men can enjoy another orgasm in about another half-hour. With the next orgasm, the muscular contractions feel pleasurable but are weaker and more irregular.

For the female, rhythmic contractions build at the outside of the vagina and move in waves down its length. The uterus contracts as well—the intensely pleasurable contractions of the vagina are repeated many times, depending on the amount of stimulation. Just before orgasm, there is feeling of tension lasting approximately three seconds as the small muscles of the pelvis surrounding the vagina and uterus contract. This is followed by a series of rhythmic muscular contractions every eight-tenths second. The series lasts for two to fifteen seconds. The feeling spreads from the outer third of the vagina backward and upward to the uterus. The average orgasm contains eight contractions. But there may be more or fewer depending on the quality of the foreplay and the current clitoral massage. A second orgasm can be experienced if excitement can be held at the plateau level. Some women can experience three or more orgasms subsequently.

The Resolution Phase

In the resolution phase, climax has come and gone, and a gradual muscular and physiological relaxation sets in for both partners. It takes about a half-hour for the various muscles to relax completely with the different swellings subsiding, skin discoloration or rashes disappearing, and organs returning to their normal sizes and positions in the body.

In men, first there is a rapid reduction in penis size. The organ shrinks to approximately 50% of its erect size during resolution phase. With the elapse of additional time, it slowly reduces to its normal length and breadth.

If ejaculation did not occur, the great amount of blood in the pelvic region will take more time to dissipate. In this case the blood will dribble out of the congested blood vessels and slowly return to the general circulation of sensation of pressure in the testes, scrotum, perineum and penis will be annoying for a time. This is the discomfort known as **Blue Balls.**

If it is allowed to happen repeatedly, blue balls will jeopardise the health of the prostate. Ejaculation results in immediate release of the tension and blood vessels engorgement in the pelvic region. Ejaculation is quite healthy.

In a woman, the nipples return to normal in the resolution phase. The excess blood drains from the vaginal lips, with the colour of the genitals returning to normal. The muscle spasm and nervous tension subside, and a great peacefulness is felt. Even so, women can easily go from the resolution to the plateau level again with some additional stimulation. Another orgasm can be reached without the waiting period necessary for males.

Orgasm allows the sudden release of blood from the pelvic blood vessels and of nerves from their heightened functioning; without this release, the return to normal takes longer.

Difference in Sexual Response Cycle

Some people prefer to prolong the arousal phase, others the plateau, some find the end of the resolution more satisfying than the tension of plateau phase or the brevity of the orgasm. For many women, physical and emotional satisfaction does not seem to be closely linked with orgasm. Coitus can be deeply satisfying even if orgasm does not occur. They enjoy pleasure from the warmth, the trust and sharing. Moreover people have different temperaments and different levels of knowledge about sex.

Normal Sexual Intercourse

Normal sexual intercourse is that which takes place between two sexually mature individuals of opposite sex. It excludes cruelty; and the use of artificial means

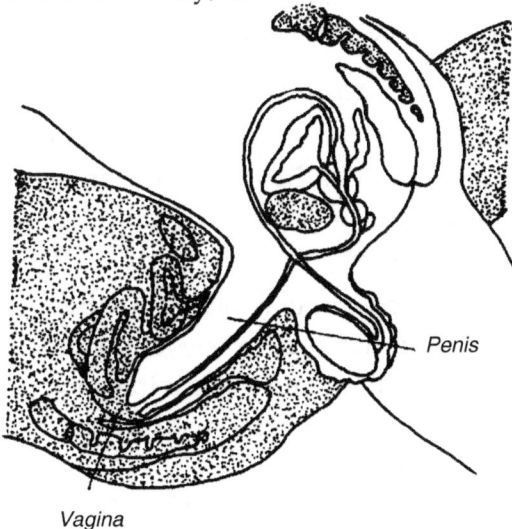

Normal Sexual Intercouse

of producing voluptious sensations. It aims directly or indirectly at the consummation of sexual satisfaction, and having achieved a certain degree of stimulation, concludes with the ejaculation or emission of the semen into the vagina at the culmination of orgasm of both partners.

When a man has sexual intercourse, his penis must be erected. For this to happen, he needs to be sexually aroused. It is possible for a woman to have sexual intercourse without being aroused. But in that case she may not enjoy it and it may be uncomfortable because the inside of her vagina would be dry.

When a man and woman have sexual intercourse, the man slides his penis inside the woman's vagina. The couple then move rhythmically together so that his penis slides up and down inside her vagina. This builds up sexual excitement until one or both of them reach orgasm. When a man has orgasm, semen spurts out of his penis. This is called ejaculation. Women do not ejaculate. Both for men and women, orgasms can be quite strong or they can be just some physical feelings in body and mind.

Tantric Way of Sexual Intercourse

A tantric believes in the transcendential power of love. Tantric love rites are Hindu sexual rites in which there is gradual progression of physical and spiritual activities culminating in orgasm.

The rite begins with the enhancement of the environment with flowers, fruit, incense, music, and candle or *deepak* light. Then comes oiling and massaging each other. Then comes bathing. Bathing is followed by meditation and *pranayama* (alternate nostril breathing known as *Nadi-Shuddhi*). Next cames humming a *mantra* during which both partners envisage themselves as *Shiva* and *Shakti*, the supreme couple. The woman then places herself to the right of the man, and the man proceeds to kiss and stroke her entire body, from toes to head and back again. She then slowly arouses her male partner with her hands and lips in a similar order. Finally the woman moves to the left of the man for the last stage of sexual fulfilment, in which various prearranged intercourse positions are employed until each of them experiences the transcendetal power of love during the climex.

Therapeutic Love Making

It refers to oriental sexual practices based on the Taoist and Tantric doctrine which propagate that specific coital postures and rhythms can have a healing effect by enabling the body to correct imbalances, for example, some positions enhance circulation of the blood, while others strengthen the bones, rest the spirit, increase the production of marrow, or adjust the whole system. Each of these benefits is believed to be achieved not only by its specific love posture but by a specific number of strokes of love by the man, as well as a specific amount of daily practice.

□□

Ideal Sexual Intercourse

An ideal and complete sexual intercourse comprises the following steps—the prelude; the love play; the sexual union; and the after play.

The Prelude

The first sign of sexual arousal in a man is usually that he has an erection because more blood flows into his penis. His testicles swell and draw up closer to his body. His penis becomes hard and erect. His body feels alive to touch, muscles start to tense up and contract. His heart starts to beat faster and shallower. His nipples may become erect and more sensitive.

In the woman more blood flows into her vulva and clitoris. Her genital area swells and feels full. Her clitoris becomes hard and erect and comes out from under its hood. She starts to produce more vaginal fluid and her labia begin to feel quite wet. Her body feels alive to touch, her muscles start to tense up and contract. Her heart starts to beat faster and her breathing becomes faster and shallower. Her nipples may become erect and more sensitive.

In some cases these changes take place slowly, in others rapidly and in exceptional instances with the speed and certainty of lightning. The prelude ends as the love play begins.

The Love Play

We can not specify any one instant of time, for terminating

the prelude and initiating the second stage. It is obvious that they merge into each other in delicate gradations. But it is not difficult to recognise. This second stage is enacted from the erotic kiss to the beginning of erotic communion. The erotic kiss is the prototype of all erotic contacts.

This particular stage in sexual relation is of special significance as it is necessary in order to excite her fully and make her ready for coital purpose. For the man who neglects the love play is guilty of coarseness and positive brutality.

Love play as an art gives a profusion of pleasures which are certainly not inferior to those of communion itself. The entire gamut of erotic activities ranging from teasing, hair pulling, caresses and kisses and all forms of physical contact that lead more or less directly to sexual gratification are parts of love play. Coquetry and flirtation are also a part of love play.

The Erotic Kiss

The erotic kiss is mutual; it is given and received from mouth to mouth with mutual pressure. This is its signature and significance. The erotic kiss may brush the bloom like a butterfly's wings in a light stroking of lips with other's pursed lips.

The tongue is indispensable in the erotic kiss and plays lead in its most important variations. The erotic kiss or French kiss is more captivating when the tip of the tongue very lightly and gently titilates the beloved's tongue and lips. Three senses are blended in the kiss—touch, taste and smell.

Love Bite

Teeth also play an important role in erotic kisses. In both from mouth to mouth and on other parts of the body.

Slight gentle bites or rather nips, which do not break the skin, express intensity of feelings. Both partners tend to use their teeth.

The normal love bite generally occurs at the more intense moments of erotic play or during coitus. The most favourite places in the man's body is the shoulder, especially the left shoulder or the place just below the collar bone. In the woman it is the neck on the left side—and the flanks of the abdomen. This selection depends in part or relatively bodily stature and positions in coitus. Women are more addicted to love bites than men. The bite occurs during coitus or immediately afterwards. Love bites are a part of love play.

Love play not only expresses itself in kisses but in touches and manual caresses also in all degrees. From gentle titilation and lighter stroking with tips of the fingers, to gripping and pressing with the palm and finger together. It may be enunciated as a rule that the lightest touches are the most effective.

Erogenous Zones

The areas of the body which make us feel sexually aroused when they are touched, stroked or kissed are called **Erogenous Zones**. These include the lips, breasts, genitals including the clitoris, vagina, penis, mouth, anus, scrotum and urethra, the areas adjacent to the sex organs and other orifices of the body like nose, ears. But no two people are alike. We find that other parts of the body make may also arouse some people when touched. These parts may be caressed depending upon individual choice.

Breasts and Nipples

Breasts and nipples have high erotic value as these are very sensitive parts. The caresses of nipples and areola, the area of the skin which surrounds the nipples if aroused by tongue, finger or by definite suction give special delight. This effect is further enhanced when the nipples themselves have become erect.

When the nipples and the clitoris are simultaneously and delicately caressed, they mutually enhance each other's stimulation. This double contact gives the maximum of possible pleasure outside coitus. Man's nipples are also capable of receiving sexual sensations and becoming erect.

The breasts are erotically very attractive. The mere sight or outline of the bosom is somewhat exciting to men; and to touch this portion of the beloved woman's body increases desire. Many women desire their breasts to be admired and fondled. Sometimes they themselves suggest. But generally speaking, the active man seems as a rule more excited by this kind of caresses than the woman who receives them.

Stimulating other Sensitive Parts

After gentle stroking and clasping of the accessory organs the hand should lightly and timidly brush the abdomen, the mons pubis, the inner side of the thighs. Alight swiftly on the sexual organ and pass at once to the other thigh.

Only by a circuitous route should it approach the holy place of sex and then tenderly seek admittance.

With these stimulations, the outer lips of the labia pout and part, revealing the clitoris and inner lips. The glands of the vestibule moisten the vulva with their special clear and slippery secretion. Thus the male's caressing hand has no difficulty in finding the vulva, and continuing its gentle endearments. These will be chiefly bestowed on clitoris. This form of contact is actually delightful to the wife and increases her desire, and the man's increases in response, as he feels her pleasure at touch.

This local stimulation, to the accompaniment of kisses and words of love, with a gradual increase in loudness of emotions, whose most effective instrument is the exchange of manipulation, continuing itself till the penis is introduced into the vagina.

With this, the finale of the love play is reached and merges into the beginning of the sexual intercourse.

The manipulation of the male organ by the female is not such an obvious and inevitable phase as the male plays a more active role than female. But a woman who has been fully initiated and possessed by the man she loves, invariably, almost automatically tries to touch and fondle his penis with her hand as soon as the erotic love play has stirred her sexually. She tries to find the most acutely sensitive spots, and applies what she knows.

It is important to know that in general, women require longer time and a wider range of stimulation than men do in order to attain to the culmination of pleasure or orgasm.

If the man receives too many powerful sensations before actual intercourse begins, then only a little more thrust is needed to bring about his ejaculation and orgasm. Local stimulation can only be occasionally necessary in the man's case.

Local stimulation may be retarded and impaired by inadequate amount of mucus secretion in the wife, owing to the poor reaction of the vestibular glands to previous bodily or psychic excitations. If lubrication is not ample, any continuous friction of the vulva, clitoris, and vagina whether during manipulation or in coitus would cause pain instead of pleasure. It would make these tender tissues so irritable and inflamed that, if the contact persists, any sexual activity would become impossible. In such cases, in the absence of natural lubrication, it must be replaced by some artificial preparation which will make the parts slippery without in itself conducing to irritation.

The most suitable genital lubricants are herbal preparations which are soluble in water and contain very few irritants. They must resemble the natural secretion which they replace.

But the most simple and obvious substitute for the inadequate lubricant is the natural moisture of the **Salivary Glands**. It is always available. As it has the disadvantage of rapid evaporation, so, it must be applied to the vulva not once but repeatedly.

Genital Kiss

The genital kiss is particularly calculated to overcome frigidity and fear in hitherto inexperienced women who have had no erotic practice, and are as yet hardly capable of specific sexual desire.

The use and enjoyment of genital kiss depends wholly on inclination, temperament, individual sensibility and practice of both the partners.

Sexual Union

Sexual union or intercourse is the third act in the love drama. It begins with the insertion of the male penis into the female vagina, and reaches culmination in the ejaculation of semen into the vagina. And also in the approximately simultaneous orgasm or summit of enjoyment in both partners. Intercourse ends when the penis is removed from the vagina. The acme of pleasure is achieved through a succession of stroking or thrusting movements.

As the penis is rubbed and pressed against the folds and pads of the vaginal walls, the nerves of the male organ, especially of its tip or glans, become so stimulated that tension is finally relieved in the sympathetic-spinal reflex discharge or ejaculation. Concurrently the increasing and overwhelming sensory impressions received by the central cortex are felt as acute pleasure. These feelings increase in force till they attain their summit in a few seconds in which ejaculation begins.

When ejaculation occurs, the pleasurable sensations continue in the form of satisfied relaxation and relief. When it ceases, the orgasm or physical discharge is at end. The psychic and physical sensations die away, into gratification—a sort of drowsy bliss.

The After Play

The afterplay is as important as foreplay. After the intense physical exertion of love making and the release of orgasm, the body finds itself in a unique state which is highly conducive to meditation and mutual absorption during which the couple should caress each other, play, talk, laugh or meditate.

Relaxation after Coitus

Many men are in the habit of going to sleep immediately after coitus. Even those men who love their wives do this due to ignorance or negligence. They turn around and start snoring while their wives feel the slow ebb of sexual longing, and thus they deprive themselves of the most exquisite psychic and emotional experience.

After intercourse, the man should help his wife to gratify her pleasure. This can be done by saying "A word of love" a kiss, a tender touch, an embrace etc. It will be enough for a loving wife to know that for him also all is not over at once. She herself desires nothing better than opportunity to prove the intense delight he has inspired in her.

Moderate Sexual Activities

As a rule, moderate sexual activity does not harm even diseased people. Normally, sexual communion has a most beneficient effect on mind and body of both partners. Especially when drowsy relaxation is followed by a short rest. It need not be actual sleep. It develops a sensation of profound gratification, of mental and physical peace, balance, self-confidence, and power which is hardly attainable in such perfection through any other experience.

The most intense and delicate happiness which human beings can taste is tasted by those couples who truly love one another.

Sexual Intercourse causes Fatigue

Normal sexual intercourse causes fatigue not because of its muscular exertion, but due to demands on nerves. The sudden relaxation after such acute tension causes not merely fatigue, but even a certain exhaustion, such as we encounter in other psychic and mental processes. The higher the tension, the more abrupt its ebb, and the more extreme the fatigue. That is why it is said—"After coitus, all creatures are sad." The sensation is drowsy, dreamy, and there is a need for sleep.

Orgasm in Women

The usual procedure is that when the man's ejaculation begins, it sets in motion the woman's acme of sensation in train at once. The time it takes for the sensation received by the woman to reach her central nervous system and translate itself into supreme delight is less than a second.

Such is the marvellous rate of nervous transmission. In normal communion the man's ejaculation gives the signal for the woman's orgasm as well as his own. The final reflex in the woman may also receive signal from her realisation of the muscular contraction of the man's orgasm.

A complete and satisfactory sexual intercourse must meet all the erotic demands of both body and soul, and should not in any way be neglected or impaired.

If the man thinks only of his own gratification as too often happens, it is stupid and cruel selfishness. Every erotic stimulation of the wife that does not terminate in orgasm on the woman's part is an injury. Such repeated injuries may cause damage to both body and mind.

A considerable number of men use **Withdrawal Method** to prevent conception. The man rapidly draws back his penis from the vagina at the moment he feels the ejaculation commence. The ejaculation therefore occurs outside the vagina. To some extent he attains relief and relaxation but it is harmful to the woman. It encourages the woman to become cold and passive.

If withdrawal is unavoidable, the man should immediately caress and stimulate his partner by genital friction and manipulation.

Stimulation through Clitoris

The small size and high position of the clitoris have special significance in coitus. Sensations caused by stimulation of the vagina are quite distinctive and dissimilar from those due to stimulation of the clitoris. In both cases there is sexual pleasure. But the sensations differ as the flavour and aroma of two fine kinds of wine.

Factors that Influence Sensation of Pleasure

The sensation of pleasure depends on the following factors:

1. Whether the stimuli are localised mainly in the *Frenulum Preputti,* these are the sebacious glands on the corona of the glans and neck of the penis or the posterior rim of glans.

2. Whether the vagina is a trifle wider or narrower.

3. Whether it is smooth or delicately folded and crinkled.

4. Whether the sensitive entrance to vagina fits the shaft of the penis closely or hardly clasps it at all.

5. Whether the tip of the penis touches the portio vaginalis or can not reach it.

6. A certain correspondence or congruence of the sexual organs of the partners is essential for ideal intercourse.

   A normal penis can no more be perfectly stimulated by an unusually wide vulva and slack vagina than can an abnormally underdeveloped or inadequately erect penis attain satisfaction by it or provide it to normal female genitalia.

But if a strong desire for sexual satisfaction has been aroused, even minor stimuli certainly suffice to cause ejaculation and a relative culmination of pleasure or atleast relief is attained. The acutest stimuli are afforded by the reciprocal pressure and friction of the penis and the vulva and vagina. But the active agent is genital and coital friction of the man. The movements of the woman are as a rule when the partners are well adapted to one another. The woman may often share the specific coital movements, by bringing her pelvis forward at the right moment and then swinging it back, thus increasing both rhythm and friction.

The Role of Love in Coitus
Physical response is indispensable to sexual connection.

Without it the man does not even get an erection. But a perfectly performed coitus demands from both partners a psycho-erotic approach which is only possible with true love. Only where love is, can the sexual pleasure be at its height, the orgasm ecstatic, the relief complete, and the drowsy and dreamy relaxation which follows a perfect peace.

The woman can begin the intercourse without special preparation but not the man. There are some changes that take place in the female genital organ during Coitus.

The flow of blood increases to the entire genital tissues. There is swelling and expansion of the bulbi the erection of the clitoris, the secretion of the vestibulary glands, the opening of the vulva, the contraction of the vaginal walls and the whole musculature of the pelvic floor. The mucus secretion flows into the vulva in preparing the vagina to receive the penis without pain.

Oral Sex

Using of mouth and tongue to kiss, lick or suck partner's genitals is called oral sex. Both men and women can become sexually aroused and have orgasm in this way. The various types of oral sex include kissing, sucking, biting, licking, exploring the partner's genital organs and erogenous zones with the tongue. A few even swallow the partner's sexual secretion.

When a man has his penis kissed, licked or sucked by a woman or someone is called *fellatio*. In Hindu manuals, it is called "playing the flute".

When a man kisses, licks or sucks a woman's genitals it is known as *cunnilingus*.

69-Position

When both partners want to lick each other at the same

time, they often adopt a position where each is coiled head to tail hence the term *Soixante neul*—a French term for 69 position. In this position *cunnilingus* and *fellatio* is performed simultaneously. It is also called *leep-de-leep*.

Frigidity

Frigidity means sexual unresponsiveness particularly in women. In medical parlance it is also known as orgastic incompetence.

In fact, this malady varies in three stages:

(a) A woman enjoys coitus but does not reach her orgasm.

(b) The woman of this category may be indifferent to sexual intercourse and she may indulge in as a part of her duty. She has no dislike for it either, but she does not enjoy it.

(c) The woman may have positive dislike for sexual intercourse and her body may "freeze" at the possibility of having it.

There are many causes for this disorder, some are psychic and some physical. Male ignorance about the subtle art of foreplay often makes a woman frigid. If the frigidity has been caused by some physical deficiency, the medical treatment is the only answer. But if the cause lies in the mind or is psychic, it is to be treated by a psychiatrist.

Vaginismus

When the muscles in woman's vagina tighten up during sexual intercourse, making it difficult for the man's penis to get into the vagina is called vaginimus. It is quite rare. A woman who has this problem should see her doctor.

Precautions to be taken During the First Night

In India, marriage is regarded as sacrosanct. It is performed with ceremony and religious rites. It is regarded as a lifelong relation and not merely a contract as is done in the west. The first-night sexual relations are named as *Suhag Raat*. This is first meeting of the married couple in privacy. It lays the foundation of the future sexual relations. The first night is supposed to be the most important event in the life of the newly married couple.

First night experience is filled with more significance for the girl than for the boy, but for both it is regarded as a religious rite in many countries. The boy has usually been taught the art of love making by his friends and elders, but for the girl the first experience of intercourse is regarded as once in a lifetime event. Therefore the husband should initiate his wife into sex gently and in the spirit of service.

In many races, religions or social rituals postponement of first intercourse for two or three days after the ceremony is prescribed. The husband should keep himself under control during the love play before the first sexual union. The prelude, with all its tender affection and admiration, kisses, embraces, gentle caresses should be given the main role. The more intensively erotic and definite stimulation should be sparingly applied.

To demand that the timid bride should yield her body suddenly and completely to the gaze of even the most beloved man, would be unreasonable and like not caring about the feelings of the bride. No woman should be expected to remove all her clothes on first night. Even to show his own erect penis to her unaccustomed eyes, would only terrify her. But every bride is not so shy and chaste.

At first night try to be natural. Talk about her hobbies, interest, subjects of choice and acquaint each other with your familial details. Never rush to consummate the marriage by physical union. Having talked and known each other, make physical advances with all its tender affection and admiration, kisses, embraces, gentle caresses should be given the main role. If you like any part of her body express your admiration by kissing that part. The women open up very gradually because a bold bride is believed to be a woman of easy virtue. The groom should be sensitive enough to judge his bride's reaction by her facial expression and gestures. Gradually arouse her sexual feelings to move towards the desired goal.

The first most important work is the defloration or the rupture of the hymen. This is located at the opening to the vagina. In fact it makes the boundry between the external and part of the genitals which develop from the skin and the internal structures of the sexual reproductive system. In some women the hymen may be more or less retained as a perforated, soft sheet of the skin, in some girls this tissue present during infancy seems to dissolve with growth, so that only slight remnants are seen as soft tags around the vaginal entrance.

In some cases the hymen is usually thick or strong. Forceful entry of a penis will overcome the obstruction. Though the woman may feel some discomfort. In rare cases, it may be necessary to consult a physician, who can snip open the hymen to allow access.

Various cultures foster the myth that all first instances of hymenal penetration are painful and show bleeding. To accomodate these expectations, women often feign pain and discomfort; To ensure the presence of blood stains; a woman or her mother may see to it that there is some blood available, perhaps from a freshly killed chicken.

In some women the pain caused by hymen rupture

interferes with the enjoyment of first coitus. But there is not always pain or even discomfort.

A newly-wed bride feels very shy and dreadful. The victory of desire over dread is often very slow and difficult. She fears of the impending pain from her torn hymen. It exists in the highest degree in the ignorant girls who know nothing about coitus or the hymental membrane. So, defloration means the beginning of the most important changes and events in a woman's life. It is the beginning of active sexual functions, with all their results, duties and dangers. In any case whether this reluctant fear be unconscious, subconscious or conscious, it should get due recognition and respect.

If the psychic preparation of the bride is incomplete, all attemps at rupture of the hymen must be deferred. The man should not begin his marriage with a rape. The woman's loss of blood from the small tears in the hymen is usually slight and soon ceases. But in exceptional cases it lasts longer and is profuse. The bride should then lie still on her back with closed legs and avoid all contact with the wound. The bleeding will stop itself. Do not dab or wipe.

At the time of intercourse if the bride does not attain full lubricant secretion to make the passage of the penis easy, an artificial lubricant should be used and applied directly to the vulva. She should be gently explained that it is meant to avoid hurting her. Then she will readily permit this, and the suggestion of consideration and care will appeal to her.

If the wife is ignorant, she must be taught, not only how to behave in coitus, but how and what to feel in this unique act; the beginning of married life is a school and an apprenticeship for her and the teacher is none other than her husband.

Sexual Awakening

The woman's sexual awakening must be gradual. It must advance step by step. The variation of attitude and positions are advanced instruction and belong to later stage.

Sexual harmony in activity is a real psychic panacea. It develops all the latent strength and sweetness of a woman's character, ripens her judgement, gives her serenity and poise.

When the woman has regular intercourse wherein full absorption of the semen takes place, the woman shows improved general and mammary development. Each such satisfactory erotic experience revives and refreshes the healthy woman throughout her soul and body.

The amount of stimulation a woman is able to receive and relief she is able to experience, depends upon her constitution, her temperament, her state of health, her psychic attitude especially on other causes of fatigue and finally on general extraneous conditions.

The sexual vigour, efficiency of the healthy, erotically awakened woman is very great, greater indeed than the potency of the average man.

Genital Classification

The Hindu treatises **Kama Sutra** and **Ananga Ranga** have given the following genital classification–

The three types of penises (*lingam*) are:

i. The **hare type** upto 13 cm long when fully erect.

ii. The **bull type** upto 18 cm long when fully erect.

iii. The **donkey type** upto 25 cm long when fully erect.

The three types of vagina (*Yoni*) are:

i. The **deer type** upto 13 cm deep.

ii. The **mare type** upto 18 cm deep.

iii. The **elephant type** upto 25 cm deep.

Types of Females

Indian love manuals mainly describe four female types:

i. The heavenly lotus woman is beautiful, soft, and full breasted and likes to make love in the daytime. They are known as **Padmini.**

ii. The artistic type woman is called **Chakrani.** She is also heavenly, beautiful and full breasted. She is proficient in the 64 arts and like to make love at night.

iii. The conch woman **Shankhni** emanates from the earthly rather than the heavenly realm. She has a large body but small breasts and is subject to sudden fits of amorous passion.

iv. The elephant type **Hastini** woman is short, stout, and slow in movement and likes prolonged love making under any and all circumstances.

Hot Spots in Women

Sexually sensitive areas are called Hot Spots. Every man should know the names of hot spots in women.

The breast

There are women whose nipples are so sensitive that they can reach orgasm when their nipples are merely caressed. Many women need simultaneous breast stimulation during the height of climatic sensation. But don't pinch or squeeze. Ask her how she likes her nipples stimulated and her breasts touched.

The pubic area

This area is also called **The Mons** and is soft and cushiony. This refers to the outside frontal part of the genitalia that is visible when a woman is in the nude.

The clitoris

The clitoris is important as a trigger in arousal and as a means toward heightening orgasmic feeling.

The outer and inner labia

The outer labia extends from the pubic area and is courser in texture than the inner labia. The inner labia extend from the clitoral hood. This tissue is highly sensitive when stroked and help in the transition from clitoral to vaginal excitation and orgasmic centering.

The vaginal opening

The first third of the entrance to the vagina is generously endowed with nerve endings. This area is also very sensitive.

The G-spot

The G-Spot is described as an area, 2 to 4 cm across, located about two fingers joint deep to the vaginal entrance. Some researchers claim that a G-Spot is very sensitive area. Its sensitivity to stimulation was first noted by the physician Grafenberg.

Hot Spots in Men

There is a male equivalent to the woman's G-Spot. Men have two **Hot Spots**. One is a nerve at the back of the penis, where the glans (head) is divided. There is also a super sensitive spot between the back of the testicles and the anal opening.

There is a deep nerve in that area which accents the degree of orgasmic sensation. If the partner will press this spot as he is about to reach a peak of sensation, he will escalate ecstasy to its extreme.

◻◻

Love Postures

A large number of coital or intercourse positions are described and illustrated in Hindu love manuals like the 4th century **Kama Sutra** and later texts such as **Ananga Ranga**.

These manuals were usually given to girls approaching puberty to prepare them for a full sexual life. Each posture is given a special name such as—Splitting a bamboo; Conjunction of Sun and Moon; Position of a cow–a dog–an elephant–a tiger–a horse–a monkey–a crab–a tortoise. Many of the positions were given poetic names such as—playing a flute which is known in the west as **Fellatio**. Tiger's tread which is known as rear entry, fluttering and soaring butterfly which is known as woman on the top position.

There are more than 200 different positions in which love making is possible. Many of these postures differ so slightly one wonders if they make any difference. Others are so complicated that passion would probably have evaporated before you got into them. Some are so twisted out of their natural shape that only an athlete can do them.

Different Postures

The main aims of different coital positions are:

1. To increase sexual pleasure, as variety is the essence of charm. Repetition of a few conventional postures tend to make sex mechanical and monotonous.

2. To prevent hygienic dangers or injuries as in the

case of pregnancy.

3. To increase the chances of conception.

    A position which facilitates ejaculation in the interior of the vagina helps the spermatozoa to penetrate into the uterus forthwith. A position of female genitals which involves depositing the semen in the immediate neigh-bourhood of the cervix, even after the cessation of the orgasm increases the likelihood of impregnation, as does also the retention of the erect penis inside the vagina.

4. To decrease the chances of conception. The chances of conception are diminished by an attitude which causes the semen to ebb back out of the vagina.

Main Positions

On can enjoy sexual intercourse standing up, sitting down, bending down or on all fours. But the basic and most common position is the **Primary Position** in which the couple is in face to face position.

It is the most common position in Western societies. It has the advantage of easy entrance and facilitation of kissing, caressing, and impregnation, but it restricts active participation on the part of the women. It is also called **Missionary Position**.

But it is not very good for the women with heavy weight partner. Nor does it allow the penis to penetrate very deeply, unless the woman puts a cushion under her bottom or raises her legs by bending her knees up or keeping her heels over her partner's shoulders.

Postures of Kama Sutra

Kama Sutra is one of the oldest love manual. It was written in 4th century by Vatsayan. The Kama Sutra is both mystical and sophisticated, and extols the sensual delights of poetry, music and perfumes. It also describes a great variety of **Intercourse Postures.**

Most of the erotic sculptures on the walls of many famous Indian temples are carved after these sexual postures of Kama Sutra of Vatsayan. Some of these positions are:

1. **Wide Open Position** *(Utfullaka)*

   Lying down on her back the woman lowers down her upper half of the body and raises back her hips. In it the entrance of the vagina is stretched wide. A pillow is placed under her back.

2. **Fixing of the Nails** *(Shaulahitaka)*

   In this posture the woman unites keeping one of her legs above her head and the other stretched out, and then holds the later up, and stretch the other and continues to do so alternatively.

3. **Crab Posture** *(Karkata)*

   In this posture both legs of the woman are folded at the knees and placed below his navel at the time of intercourse.

4. **Yawning Position** *(Vijrimbhitaka)*

   In this position the woman raises her thighs and keeps them wide apart and unites.

5. **Pressing Posture** *(Piditaka)*

   In this posture both the lovers begin in clasping position, and then they press each other's thigh with force.

6. **The Twining Position** *(Veshtika)*

   In this position the woman unites with the man in the clasping position, places her left thigh on the right in order to contract her vagina even more.

7. **The Mare Position** *(Vadavak)*

   In this position the woman hold the man's penis firmly in her vagina as does the mare.

8. **Splitting of the Bamboo** *(Venudaritaka)*

   In this position the woman places one of her legs on the man's shoulder, and keeps the other stretched out.

9. **The Lotus Posture** *(Padamasan)*

   In this posture the right foot of the woman is on the left thigh, and the left foot on the right thigh.

10. **Supported Congress** *(Sthirrata)*

    In this posture both man and woman support each other against a wall or a pillar, and involve themselves in sexual intercourse.

11. **Congress of A Cow** *(Dhenuka)*

    In this posture the woman gets down on her all fours like a cow, and the man mounts on her from behind like a bull.

12. **The United Congress** *(Sanghatak)*

    In this posture a man enjoys two women simultaneously.

13. **Congress of the Herd of Cows** *(Gauyuthika)*

    When a man enjoys several women at the same time.

    ⬜⬜

Common Questions for Adolescents

Q.1 Why do people have sex?

Ans. The term sex is derived from the Latin word *sexus*, which means to cut or to divide. Sex is the natural way of ensuring the continuation of species. Animals never think about it, they only respond to chaning levels of sex hormones which stimulate the reproductive urge. But as far as human beings are concerned it is made complicated by thoughts and feelings. We have sex because it gives us pleasure. Sex is the center of a loving relationship, a true bond between two people. The basic sex drive is a universal experience, but what turns people on differes from culture to culture. The rules and customs which govern sexual behaviour vary enormously from place to place.

Q.2 Why do people feel embarrassed while discussing sex?

Ans. Sex has been associated for so long with unacceptable and dirty feelings. Embarrassment also comes from the secrecy surrounding the sexual act. Our religious preachers always preach to abstain from sex and observe abstinence to attain salvation. A *brahamchari* is respected in the Hindu society. But in societies where sex has been open and free from ideas of guilt, it is accepted much more easily as being normal and natural.

Q.3 Why do boys enjoy looking at the pictures of naked women?

Ans. Generally boys and men can become sexually aroused when looking at pictures of naked women, blue films and by having sexual fantasies. Sexual arousal is a pleasurable feeling. So they enjoy looking at such type of materials.

Q.4 If any boy or girl is not very interested in sex, are they normal?

Ans. There is no fixed age when boys or girls suddenly become interested in sex. The way they feel has a lot to do with the level of sex hormones which are estrogens in girls and testotrones in boys. As the primary sex characteristics and organs produce more hormones, awareness of sexuality will gradually increase and then you will also become aware of the sexuality of others. Physical features directly involved in sexual behaviour and reproduction: the gonads (testes and ovaries) and the external sex organs (penis and vagina) are known as primary sex characteristics.

Q.5 Are the girls who carry contraceptives promiscuous?

Ans. Promiscuity is a casual and unselective sexual relation with a variety of partners, often without obtaining full sexual satisfaction. But this does not apply to the girl who carries contraceptives. Frankly speaking she is accepting responsibility for her actions. She cares both for herself and her boyfriends.

Q.6 If a girl feels sexy for more than one boy at a time,

does it mean she is nymphomaniac?

Ans. Nymphomania is a compulsive, insatiable need for sexual stimulatin and gratifucation in women, frequently leading to promiscuity or to masturbation performed several times a day. But in this case it simply means that she is young and healthy. Hormone activity around puberty makes a young person feel very sexually excited at times.

Q.7 If you want to have sex with someone, are you in love?

Ans. Love and sex are two different things. You do not have to be in love to be turned on by someone. People are often drawn to each other sexually, even though they know they could never really love each other. After puberty boys and girls begin to develop their own sexuality. They may find themselves attracted to other people, like their classmates, friends, teachers and even complete strangers. This intensity of feeling may be overwhelming. It takes time and experience to adjust to these new emotions.

Q.8 What type of sex is wrong?

Ans. It depends upon person's own attitude towards sex in general. There is no check-list. The only hard and fast rule is that sex must always be voluntary and never be violent No one should force something on the other.

Q.9 Why do people have sex with prostitutes?

Ans. The are many reasons why people go to prostitutes. They may be feeling lonely, or trapped in an unhappy marriage, They may not want emotional involvement in their sexual relationship or just for pleasure.

Q.10 What is sexual perversion?

Ans. Sexual perversion is that sexual behaviour which is culturally, morally and legally unacceptable. In simple words, it is the sexual behaviour which is extreme and anti-social, also these unusual sexual activities would shock or offend most people.

Q.11 What is sexual harassment?

Ans. It refers to repeated and unwanted sexual comments, looks, suggestion or physical contact which make one feel uncomfortable. It is very common throughout the world.

Q.12 Why do girls have periods?

Ans. A Periods or menstruation is the discharge of blood and tissue from the lining of the uterus, which has been built up in anticipation of implantation of a fertilized egg. It is a unique plan of nature for reproduction. Through this method the uterus is made ready each month for pregnancy. If conception does not take place and the egg is not fertilized, this lining breaks down and together with a small amount of blood, it is shed in the menstrual period.

The blood that comes out of vagina is not a sign that anything is wrong. A girl starts to menstruate when she begins puberty. This can be any time between the age of 9 and 18. The average age is about 13. The number of days between each period is governed by the production of hormones and this varies from person to person. Very few girls have completely regular periods. Although it is inconvenient to have irregular periods, but it is not abnormal.

During this period many girls and women feel discomfort, tension and irritability. It is a good idea to use a tampon or a sanitary towel for extra protection. This is a particular good time to exercise.

Q.13 What is clitoris and where is it?

Ans. clitoris is the most sensitive part of the female genitals. Girls may be less aware of their sexual organs than boys because their external organs are smaller and less obvious. Clitories is full of nerve endings. When stimulated it becomes stiff like an erect penis and pokes out of its hood. Stimulating the clitoris helps many women to have an orgasm.

Q.14 What is orgasm?

Ans. Orgasm is the peak or climax of sexual excitement and pleasure during which ejaculation of semen occurs in the male and vicinal contraction in the female. The peak period lasts less than one minute for most males and females. To have an orgasm you need to be sexually aroused. Your clitoris or penis needs to be rubbed and stimulated until the feeling of pleasure and sexual tension becomes very strong. At orgasm this tension is suddenly released. This can send waves of intense pleasure through your whole body. Men experience orgasm more often than women.

Q.15 Can any girl make her breasts grow bigger?

Ans. There is nothing one can do to hasten the growth of breasts. If anyone tries to sell you creams guaranteed to increase breast size then he is taking you for a ride. Exercise is also no help either since there are no muscles in the breast tissue itself. The size of the breasts makes no difference when you become pregnant. During pregnancy, the glands become larger to prepare for lactation.

Q.16 Do all men ejaculate?

Ans. All men do not ejaculate. There are physical and psychological reasons why some men are unable to ejaculate. In their case, the unused sperms just disintegrate and are absorbed harmlessly into the body. Ejaculation is not possible without erection. Erection usually provides the signals needed for ejaculation.

Q.17 Can I do something to stop erection when there are other people around?

Ans. Sometimes boys have erection at the most unexpected and awkward moments. Not only thought of a girl or sight of a girl but intense emotions like fear or anger and even strenuous physical exercise may give you an erection. In such a situation distract yourself by thinking of something that takes your mind off it. That is why there is a joke that penis have an annoying habit of becoming erect at the wrong time and refusing to erect at the right time.

Q.18 Do semen and pee ever get mixed?

Ans. Semen never comes out when you pee as there is a special valve value which automatically shut of urine when the penis is erect.

0.19 Why do boys and girls masturbate?

Ans. Masturbation helps relieve some of the sexual tension that is an inevitable part of growing up. Both boys and girls masturbate. Boys masturbate more than girls because the penis is more accessible and they are more used to touching it.

Masturbation is not bad for health in anyway. But always remember that masturbation should not become compulsive.

Girls and women masturbate mostly with their hands, rubbing against the sensitive ,clitoris at the top of the vulva. They may use a firm action over the whole vulva. Sometime using one or more fingers to enter the vagina and mimic the rhythmic movements of intercourse.

Q.20 What causes erection?

Ans. It is some kind of sexual signal which causes the penis to become erect. Sometimes it is caused by an erotic photograph or by the sight of a pretty girl; sometimes just the thought of a girl or of love making is enough to make it happen. But morning erection, commonly experienced by men upon awakening, is usually because of the pressure of a full bladder.

Q.21 Who is impotent?

Ans. A man who is unable to have an erection or to maintain it long enough to have sex is termed as impotent. It is a psychological problem which depends upon various factors. If a boy has had, a bad experience with a girl, he may not be able to have an erection the next time he tries to have sex.

Q.22 What is a condom?

Ans. A condom is a thin rubber sheath which unrolls to fit over a man's erect penis. It can be used during sexual intercourse between a man and a woman. It helps prevent the woman from becoming pregnant and lowers the risk of sexually transmitted infection.

A condom must be put on before the penis touches vaginal area of the woman and it must be kept on until the penis is fully out of the vagina. A condom can only be used once. After it has been used, it should be wrapped in a tissue and throw in a dust bin. With a little practice, condoms are easy to use. They can be bought from a chemist shop and they are freely distributed at Family Planning Centres.

Condoms are safe, but they need to be used carefully. A tear in the condom could be disastrous. Make sure no air gets trapped when the condom is rolled over the erect penis.

Q.23 Why is it advised to consult a doctor before using a pill?

Ans. The contraceptive pill contains the female hormones estrogen and progesterone. They are designed to prevent ovulation by stopping the ova (eggs) from maturing in the ovaries. As it contains powerful hormones which interrupt the normal monthly cycle. Women should only take it under medical supervision. The doctor can keep a watch on its side effects.

Q.24 What is sterilisation?

Ans. It is a permanent method of contraception for both

men and women. Sterilisation makes the person sterile so they cannot start a baby.

Male sterilisation is called vasectomy. It involves closing off both of the vasdeferens so that sperm cannot travel into the man's urethra and out of his penis. After this operation, the person can still have erections, ejaculate and enjoy sex in the same way that he did before he was sterilised.The only difference is that now his semen contains no sperms. It is a very tiny operation taking only about 15 minutes. It is done under local anaesthesia, so there is no pain. Our Government is encouraging this method of family planning by offering a number of incentives.

Female sterilisation involves closing off both fallopian tubes so that ova cannot travel into the uterus. This means that the woman cannot get pregnant. But she still has menstural periods and she can enjoy sex in the same way that she did before she was sterilied.

But these are suitable only for those who are absolutely sure that they don't want any more children and that they won't change their mind later on.

Q.25 How would you know if you are pregnant or not?

Ans. To find out whether you are pregnant or not, go to a doctor or hospital or any family planning clinic. Pregnancy test cannot be done until 14 days after your last period was due. If the test is positive, you are pregnant. A negative result is not a clear signal. You will need to wait another four or five days and then have yourself tested again to be absolutely sure.

Q.26 What is AIDS?

AIDS stands for Acquired Immune Deficiency Syndrome. If you have AIDS, your body's immune system breaks down and it cannot fight off infections. AIDS is caused by a virus called HIV. You cannot catch AIDS but you can be infected with HIV. Experts think that most people with HIV eventually get HIV related symptoms or AIDS.

The two main ways in which this disease is passed on are:

- By direct sexual contact.
- By getting infected blood into your blood stream.

  You cannot catch the virus from toilet seats or from things like utensils or towels used by an AIDS victim. This deadly virus is known to be transmitted from the mother to the unborn child in the womb or at birth. or to a baby through the mother's milk.

Q.27 What is rape?

Ans. When any man forces another person (usually a woman) to have sexual intercourse against her will, it is known as rape. The man who rapes someone is called a rapist. Rape is a horrible crime. It is usually violent and very frightening for the person being raped. The victim is often known to the rapist.

Q.28 What is oral sex?

Ans. Oral sex is a general term for use of the lips, mouth, tongue and throat cavity in sexual stimulation and gratification. The various types of oral sex include kissing, sucking, biting, licking, exploring the partner's genital organs and erogenous zones with the tongue and swallow the partner's sexual secretions. when a woman has her genitals kissed, licked or sucked by someone, it is called cunnilingus. When a man has his penis kissed, licked or sucked by someone, it is called fellatio. There is a very small risk of catching HIV through oral sex. That is the reason why it has become so popular in these days.

Q.29 Are wet dreams harmful in any way?

Ans. Wet dreams are not harmful in any way. They are only a sign that your reproductive organs are developing and they can happen quite often during puberty. But don't worry if you don't have them because that is normal too.

Q.30 What is the thr-eoctrine Signature?

Ans. Throughout the world many people still believe that outward appearace of a substance represents its inner concept. Certain objects that outwardly resemble sexual organs are believed to have aphrodisiac effects. Examples are Rhinoceros Horn or Oyster that resemble penis and vagina respectively. Olives represent testes and cooked Okara represents vaginal lubrication.

An aphrodisiac is that substance that is alleged to stimulate sexual desire and activity. It is possible that suggestion plays a major part when they appear to have an effect.

Q.31 What are the effects of antisex indoctrination?

Ans. Antisex indoctrination is the instilling of negative attitude towards sex, especially in children. Many parents as a result of their own inhibitions, hangups or religious belief raise their children in a cool atmosphere in which cuddling, caressing and touching are discouraged or even punished. They keep their children in total ignorance of sexual matters and oppose sex education not only at home but in school too. These attitudes lay the ground work for sexual conflicts. frigidity and impotence in many instances.

Q.32 Why do some people feel inadequate while doing sex?

Ans. A person may be a millionaire, a world leader, an athlete, a wrestler or a distinguished scientist but may still feel inadequate doing a simple act of sex that is common for animals and birds.

It is because animals and birds never think about it. They just respond to changing levels the of sex hormones which stimulate or curb their reproductive urge. But in the case of men and women, instincts have been crippled by anxiety resulting from negative preconditioning normally based on expectations of family and society.

Q.33 What is sexual rejuvination?

Ans. Sexual rejuvination is the restoration of youthful sexual vigour among the ageing. An untold number of substances exercises and treatments have been tried but found wanting. Among them are downright frauds like radio-active water, X-ray lamps and various pills and potions.

Q.34 What is sex counselling?

Ans. Sex counselling is the guidance provided to an individual or couple by a sex therapist, social worker, psychiatrist, or doctor on questions such as conception, family planning, infertility, fear of failure in performance, unresponsiveness, sexual anatomy and physiology and techniques of intercourse.

Q.35 What is the sex centre of the brain?

Ans. Sex centre of the brain is a term sometimes applied to a small area at the base of the brain which is believed to control the sex drive and various sexual functions, including the ovulation cycle in the female and ejaculation in the male. Its principal component is the pituitary gland, the MASTER GLAND that programs not only the sex glands but every other gland in the body. Studies have also suggested that damage in this area may be one of the causes of nymphomania and satyriasis on the one hand and impotence and diminished sex interest on the other hand.

Satyriasis is a male sexual disorder characterised by an obsessive insatiable desire for sexual gratification. Nymphomania is a compulsive insatiable need for sexual stimulation and gratification in women, frequently leading to promiscuity or to masturbation performed several times a day.

◻◻

SELF-IMPROVEMENT/PERSONALITY DEVELOPMENT

Also Available
in Hindi

Also Available
in Hindi

Also Available
in Kannada, Tamil

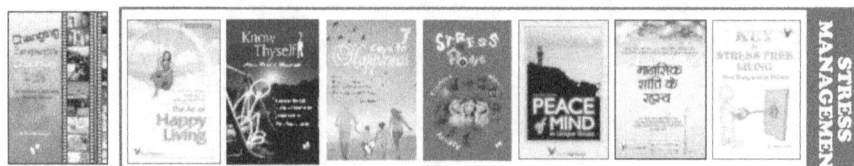

Also Available
in Kannada

Also Available
in Kannada

STRESS MANAGEMENT

All books available at www.vspublishers.com

Also Available
in Hindi, Kannada

Also Available
in Hindi, Kannada

Contact us at sales@vspublishers.com